CROSSWORD PUZZLES FOR KIDS

AGES 7 & UP

Woo! jr
KiDS activities

Copyright © 2017, Woo! Jr. Kids Activities / Wendy Piersall. All rights reserved.

Woo! Jr. Kids Activities Founder: Wendy Piersall
Production Coordinator: Cassidy Piersall
Cover Illustration: Michael Koch | Sleeping Troll Studios www.sleepingtroll.com

Published by:
Wendybird Press
1151 Lake Ave.
Woodstock IL, 60098
www.wendybirdpress.com

ISBN-13: 978-0997799309
ISBN-10: 0997799307

wendybird
press

How to Play Crosswords!

Use the clues to guess the correct words to fill the puzzle! Use written clues, number of letters, and previous answers to get the solutions.

Sometimes the answer to a clue will be two words, like "Word Puzzle" above. These written clues will be marked with a **(2)**.

STUMPED?
The answer keys for all the puzzles in this book can be found at:
http://www.woojr.com/kids-crossword-answers/

Fri. Jun 12 2020

Animal Sounds!

Across

2. Cats like to purr and Meow
4. Frogs and toads like to croak and cricet
6. Something a duck or goose might say!
7. You might hear this sound from a chicken.
8. This is a sound a large animal, such as a dog or tiger, makes when it's mad.

Down

1. A sound likely to come from an owl.
3. This is the noise a pig makes.
5. What does a dog say when it's happy?
7. Was that a bird?

Art!

Across
2. Some people create art with a lot of _____, like a story that helped inspire it or a reason it was made.
3. _____ is fun to use when making art because you can use it with your fingers or a brush.
4. Some people create art using ____, making ceramic pieces that can then be painted or glazed if desired.
7. Sometimes it is tough to find _____ when you want to create art, but just don't know what you want to do.

Down
1. Making art can be very _____ and stress reducing.
3. A large _____ of colors is great to have because it gives you more options.
5. For some, creating art is ____. For others, it is their hobby.
6. While some art is black and white, others are full of different _____.

At the Beach!

Across
2. Beach ___s are fun things to have at the beach because they are full of air and bounce easily.
4. Most beaches are made of this. Billions of tiny rocks everywhere!
6. This can be motorized or moved with oars.
7. Simple shoes worn during the summer that have straps across your feet separating your big toe from the rest.

Down
1. This is crafted from sand, water and plastic molds, or even just your hands! (2 words)
3. A bathing _____ is worn when you plan on getting in the water.
4. These are very nice to wear when it is super bright and sunny.
5. A long piece of fabric used to dry your body off.

Autumn!

Across
2. A famous sport that is played through autumn and into the winter in the U.S.A.
4. A popular fruit to pick from a tree that can be made into a pie.
6. The holiday of November.
7. Halloween is the perfect time to _____ pumpkins!

Down
1. The main holiday of October.
3. Huge and orange, this plant is commonly hollowed out, carved and decorated.
5. _____ is a tasty, warm drink that is made from apples.

BaBies!

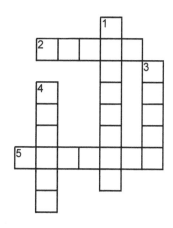

Across

2. Since babies are not born with _____, they need to be fed soft foods before they eat solid foods.
5. Babies are constantly going through _____ because they are not potty trained yet.

Down

1. This is used to push babies around for transportation instead of carrying them.
3. These disappear even faster than diapers, and are used to clean baby bottoms.
4. Babies spend a lot of time _____ because they can't communicate with words.

BaBy Animals!

Across

3. A baby frog.
4. A baby cow, camel or dolphin.
5. A baby goat; can also refer to a young human.
6. Refers to many newly born primates, such as a human, gorilla, and baboon.

Down

1. A baby dog and the word for many newborn rodents.
2. A baby bird that has just hatched is called this.
5. A baby cat.

Backyard!

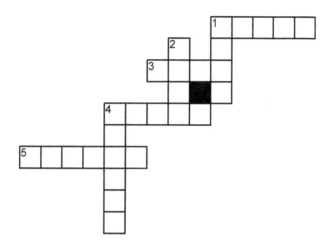

Across
1. This is fun to sway back and forth on!
3. You use this to water the garden or fill a pool.
4. This is used to cook food outdoors, like steak, hamburgers, chicken, or hot dogs.
5. These are likely to be sitting on your patio, deck, or right outside the door for people to sit on.

Down
1. This is where a family might store things like the lawn mower and summer supplies.
2. Not everyone has one, but those that do can go swimming any time!
4. This is full of flowers or vegetables.

In the Bathroom!

Across

1. This is where you wash your hands.
5. You use this to clean your teeth, along with a toothbrush.

Down

1. You can take a _____ instead of a bath.
2. Sometimes you might take a _____ instead of a shower.
3. This is what you use to wash your hands.
4. This is in every single bathroom. It is used for "going to the bathroom".
5. This is often kept hanging or folded up until you use it to dry off.

Birds!

Across

2. This is intensely colorful and can learn to talk!
4. This bird can flap its wings up to 50 times per second, creating a "hum" sound.

Down

1. The largest bird in the world; their eggs can weigh up to 3 pounds each.
2. A small species of parrot, commonly kept as a pet.
3. A scavenger bird found in Africa that feeds off of animal carcasses.

Things That Are Blue!

Across
3. Over 95% of the all the water on Earth is found in the _____s.
4. A pretty bird! (2 words)
5. This is a gemstone.

Down
1. A _____'s egg is unique because the shell is blue!
2. A small fruit.
5. On a bright, cloudless day, the ___ is very blue.

On a Boat!

Across

3. This floats in the water as a marker and will also keep a boat from bumping into a dock.
5. You should always wear a ____ _____ (2 words) when on a boat, just to be safe. This would save you from drowning!
6. This is worn on your head and can keep your face from getting a sunburn.

Down

1. This is something you can spray or rub on your skin to protect it from getting sunburned.
2. You wear these on your feet in the summer.
4. This is worn when you plan on swimming or getting wet.

Boom!

Across
3. This is a bright, sparkly thing you would see in the sky on the 4th of July.
5. A violent burst of flames.

Down
1. This is what an exploded star is called.
2. These were weapons used on pirate ships to shoot large metal balls in the air.
4. A sound that occurs when an object travels through the air faster than the speed of sound. (2 words)

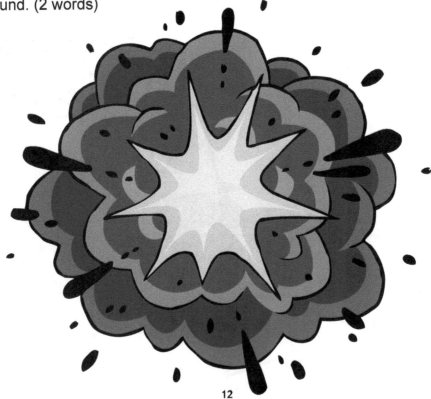

Body Parts!

Across
3. You use these to write.
5. You might wear rings on these.
6. You use these to hear.

Down
1. You use this to smell.
2. This is where your leg bends.
3. This pumps blood through your body.
4. These are what you breathe with!

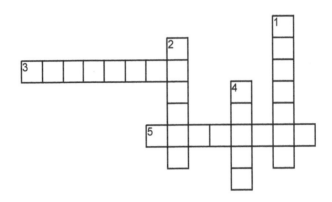

Breakfast!

Across

3. This is a way of cooking eggs that requires additional ingredients such as bacon, veggies, or cheese, and is folded in half before serving.
5. When you eat these, they often come in stacks of 2 or more. Don't forget butter and syrup!

Down

1. This unique breakfast food is very similar to pancakes, however, these have a distinct shape with a crisp outside.
2. This is served in a bowl with milk.
4. This is simply a warm and crisped slice of bread.

14

Bugs & Insects!

Across
3. No one likes this bug! It loves to leave super itchy spots on you and can carry diseases.
4. This insect isn't gross or scary like others! Its wings can be many different colors when it emerges from a cocoon.
5. This arachnid spins large webs in order to catch its prey.

Down
1. Sometimes this crawling bug can get into your home if food is left out.
2. When this is nearby, you might hear a buzzing sound. This flying, furry insect is yellow and black and might sting you if it gets upset.

On the calendar!

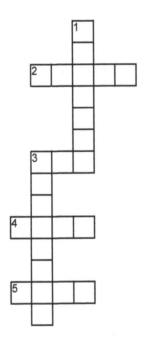

Across

2. 12 per year.
3. 365 per year.
4. A _____ is how long it takes for Earth to orbit the Sun.
5. There are 7 days in a _____.

Down

1. The first month of the year.
3. The last month of the year.

Camping!

Across

3. One of the first things you do when you go camping is set up or "pop" your _____.
4. People love to tell _____ around a campfire with good friends.
5. This is not the easiest to start, but it will keep you very warm.
6. Once it gets dark out, it's very handy to have a _____ with you so that you can see your surroundings.

Down

1. When it's time to go to sleep, you unzip and climb into your _____ ____ so that you are warm. (2 words)
2. On a clear night, you can lay under the _____ and admire the whole universe!
4. The ultimate camping dessert! All you need is a fire, stick, marshmallows, chocolate and graham crackers.

In the car!

Across

2. This is a special safety seat for younger children to sit in. (2 words)
3. It is very important to wear a _____ _____. It could save your life in an accident! (2 words)
5. These will burst out of various places of your car in a collision to help prevent injury.
6. This is a large space in the back of your car for storage.

Down

1. A _____ is nice to have when you want to listen to music.
2. A spot just for your drink! (2 words)
4. If a driver breaks the law, they will get pulled over by police and will receive a _____.

cats!

Across

3. A cat with the word "cat" in its name; it is about the size of a dog.
4. Another name for a domesticated cat that lives indoors. (2 words)
5. A large orange and white cat with black stripes.

Down

1. King of the jungle.
2. A large and fast cat; also a car brand.

chores!

Across

2. Clean clothes are only available when someone has done the _____.
4. In the fall, thousands of _____ will fall from the trees and they need to get raked up.
5. In school, you often get extra work to do at home to bring back and turn in to your teacher.

Down

1. For some this is a chore, for some it is a job or hobby. Either way, after doing some _____, your yard might have new plants or flowers.
2. It is important to change and/or clean the cat _____ box so it doesn't get smelly.
3. Doing the _____ is important so that you have clean utensils and plates on which to eat meals.

Christmas!

Across

3. These appear under your tree on Christmas morning.
5. This is who gives gifts to all the kids of the world!
6. This is what all the presents are covered with. (2 words)

Down

1. The day before. (2 words)
2. This is who the celebration is really about!
4. The biggest shopping day of the season - the day after Thanksgiving. (2 words)

Types of clothing!

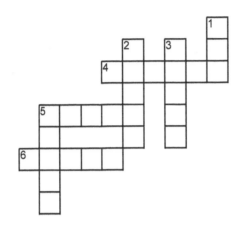

Across

4. This is heavier than a shirt, but lighter than a coat.
5. This can have long, short or no sleeves.
6. For your feet, between you and your shoes.

Down

1. Wear this on your head.
2. Wear these on your legs.
3. A bottom with no division between the legs.
5. For your feet.

Common Allergies!

Across

3. This allergy commonly irritates people in the springtime when plants start to bloom.
4. These can be cooked many different ways - sunny-side up, over easy, scrambled, or hard boiled.

Down

1. You are probably allergic to this if you are itchy & sneezy around pets like cats, dogs and horses.
2. If you can't have this, it means you are lactose intolerant and must avoid dairy products.
3. An allergy that would stop someone from eating PB&J's.

CUDDly Looking Animals!

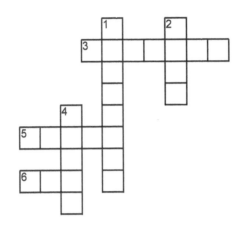

Across

3. This is a flightless bird that lives in very cold weather.
5. This furry animal appears to be extremely lazy and very slow-moving.
6. This bird says "hoot"!

Down

1. This cute pet looks like a mini porcupine.
2. This bird is often found in ponds during the summer time.
4. Often referred to as a _____ bear, this is not actually a bear but rather a marsupial from Australia.

Dangerous Animals!

Across

3. An extremely venomous snake that will shake its tail to warn other animals to keep away.
5. This lays eggs, has the feet of an otter, bill/face of a duck, tail of a beaver, is venomous and is actually a mammal!
6. Commonly referred to as a "croc", and sometimes mistakenly called an alligator.

Down

1. This is the fourth largest land animal in the world. It has tusks inside its mouth and can open its jaws extremely wide.
2. Unique marine creatures with a mushroom or umbrella shaped top and lots of tentacles that can sting you.
4. This is a type of snake that kills its prey through constriction.

Days of the week!

Across
4. Three days after Monday.
5. The day after the last day of the week.
6. The first weekday of the week.

Down
1. The middle of the week - hump day!
2. The last weekday.
3. The last day of the week.
4. Two days before Thursday.

In the Desert!

Across

2. This mammal is known for the humps on its back, which help it survive in the hot desert.
4. Dehydration is dangerous and you are not likely to find much _____ in the desert.
5. These are prickly, so don't touch them!
6. These are closely related to spiders, however they have stingers at the ends of their tails and a tiny pair of claws in front.

Down

1. These will be quick to bite you if you don't stay away, especially when you hear their tail rattling.
3. It's everywhere, just like at a beach!

Desserts!

Across
4. This is frequently eaten for breakfast and shaped like a cupcake.
5. Often comes in a cone. (2 words)
6. This is great to dunk in milk.

Down
1. A tiny cake!
2. A slice of this is especially yummy when apple or pumpkin flavored.
3. On your birthday, you might stick candles into one of these.

At the Dinner Table!

Across
2. The main _____ for a meal is often the largest portion or highlight.
3. This is sometimes "placed" under your plate!
4. _____ and _____ go perfectly together to add flavor from shakers. (2 words)
5. This is what you eat your food off of. It can be made of paper, plastic, glass, or pottery.

Down
1. This is what you eat your food with. They come in different shapes for cutting, scooping and picking up food.

At the Doctor's Office!

Across

5. This is administered for a variety of reasons. You might get one to receive a vaccine, to prevent allergies, or to be anesthetized.
6. This will cause you to lose feeling wherever it is given.

Down

1. You should go to the _____ _____ if you are in immediate danger of dying - like suffering from a car accident or heart attack. (2 words)
2. You are likely to be visited by a _____ when at the doctor's office.
3. Whose office?
4. This is where you go if you need the emergency room, to have surgery done, or for other medical reasons.
5. Sometimes you go to the doctor for a simple check-up, but other times it may be because you are ____.

Don't Want That!

Across
3. Whether it's a bee, wasp or another bug, nobody likes to get _____!
5. Make sure you wear lots of sunscreen or sunblock! Otherwise you will end up with a red and painful _____.
6. If you need to catch a bus or train, make sure you arrive early so you don't _____ it!

Down
1. Running a red light, stop sign, or not paying attention to the road is likely to cause a car _____.
2. If your mom or dad happens to drive over a nail or other sharp object, there is a good chance of getting a _____ _____. (2 words)
4. If you get hit or bump into something too hard, you might end up with a _____.

Things to Drink!

Across

5. The perfect drink to have with breakfast! This cold drink sometimes has floating pulp from the fruit it's made from. (2 words)
6. This drink can be hot or cold. It's just water with some herbs!

Down

1. Adults like to drink this in the morning or when they want to stay awake.
2. A fruit juice drink often made in the fall/winter. A touch of cinnamon is yummy! (2 words)
3. You couldn't live without this one! In fact, more than half your body is made of this.
4. A drink that is used with many foods. You might drink it with breakfast or pour it into your cereal.

Emergency!

Across

3. In the event of a tornado or severe thunderstorm, it may be necesary to take _____ in a basement or stairwell.
4. If you have already been harmed, it is very important to find a _____ ___ kit to bandage yourself up. (2 words)
5. In tremendous circumstances, you may need to _____ in order to completely avoid danger.

Down

1. If there is immediate danger nearby, like a criminal or a tornado, you should ask the nearest _____ what to do to be safest, whether that is a parent, teacher, or police officer.
2. If there is an emergency, you should call the _____ immediately.

Emotions!

Across

3. Monsters, horror movies and the dark are all things that people are commonly _____ of.
5. _____ is what people feel if they are deceived or if they are in an argument.
7. When something suddenly happens that you were not expecting, you might be a little _____.

Down

1. What everyone wants to feel!
2. Lots of people feel _____ when they have to talk in front of crowds.
4. Bullies often make people feel ___.
6. You will probably feel _____ when you show your mom or dad you got an A+ on your test!

EnDangereD Animals!

Across
5. A powerful, surprisingly fast and massive animal that can weigh 3,000 lbs. When they open their mouths, you can see their tusks.
6. A big, orange cat with black stripes.

Down
1. A unique African animal with large horns in the middle of its face.
2. A type of ape found north of the Congo River in Africa, often abbreviated to "chimp".
3. The largest animal on land, this animal has a very large trunk and some have tusks.
4. A black and white bear that lives in parts of China.

Family!

Across
3. Your parent's sibling's kid.
7. Your parent's male parent.
8. A male parent.
9. Your parent's female parent.

Down
1. The sister of your mother or father.
2. A female parent.
4. A female sibling.
5. A male sibling.
6. The brother of your mother or father.

On a Farm!

Across

3. A baby _____ is referred to as a lamb.
6. An animal you can saddle up and ride.
7. This is a huge, motorized vehicle that is used for various tasks around a farm.

Down

1. What came first, the _____ or the egg?
2. This might outline the whole farm, especially around areas for animals to keep them separate from others, or contained on the property.
4. The offspring of this animal is called a kid.
5. This is common to have on farms - it often holds animals indoors.

places to find clocks!

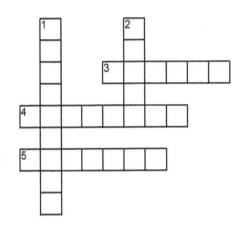

Across
3. This is a famous clock tower in London, England. (2 words)
4. This is what you use to surf the internet at a desk.
5. These are similar to computers, but they look like large smart phones.

Down
1. This is used to cook food quickly.
2. If someone is wearing a watch, they can tell the time by looking at their _____.

Fish!

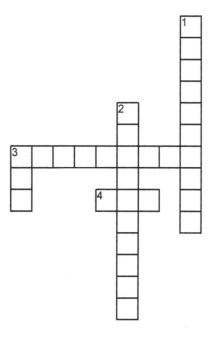

Across
3. A "funny" fish that is orange with white stripes and lives in anemones.
4. This kind of fish can be "electric"; it has a long, snake-like body.

Down
1. The _____ _____ shark is one of the largest predators in the ocean. (2 words)
2. This fish puffs up to protect itself.
3. This fish is commonly eaten as fish sticks or fish and chips.

Flowers!

Across

2. Another word for mom; this flower has many petals.
3. A deep red flower with a thorny stem.
5. A weed that you blow on to make a wish!
6. Perfect white petals around a bright yellow center.

Down

1. Big & yellow - the size of the "sun"!
4. A mean word to call someone who is afraid.

Fruits!

Across

4. This fruit is a berry that is hollow with an open top.
6. A super sour fruit, too sour to eat alone! It tastes great in a cup of ice water or tea.
7. A small blue fruit.

Down

1. A big yellow and green tropical fruit that can be a little sour and has rough, prickly skin.
2. A red fruit with lots of seeds covering the outside.
3. This fruit tastes great with peanut butter and is made into cider in autumn!
5. This fruit is named after its color!

Gardening!

Across

3. Some people add stepping _____ to their garden so they can move through it without walking all over their hard work.
6. Fill your garden with these if you love wonderful smells and lots of color.
7. When the lawn needs to be ___, it's important to only get the grass and not the garden!
8. These edibles are not always sweet, but they are very good for you. Many grow underground.

Down

1. A useful tool! This will help you plant large plants deep in the ground.
2. Nobody likes these. When you're working in the garden, sometimes you have to take time to remove these pesky plants.
4. Plant these to eat! They are sweet treats to pick. Many grow on trees.
5. A good pair of _____ should protect you from thorns or splinters.

Gemstones!

Across
3. This stone is a pretty purple shade.
4. Most commonly used in wedding rings, this stone is clear.
5. Often cut into rectangles, this stone is bright green.

Down
1. This stone is a bright, deep and bold red color.
2. This stone is a bold and striking blue color.
3. This stone is a lighter shade of blue.

Girly Stuff!

Across
4. If a girl practices ballet, she is called a _____.
5. Not every girl likes the color _____, but it is considered a girly color.
6. While some boys participate in this athletic group activity, you'll find mostly girls encouraging sports teams with chants and dances from the sidelines.

Down
1. Lots of girls will _____ their hair with a hot iron for special occasions.
2. Girly movies that are typically funny and romantic are called _____ _____s. (2 words)
3. Some girls love getting a _____, the word for having your nails done.

Government!

Across

3. A _____ is a person who makes a decision in court based on the law, evidence presented, and without bias.
5. An _____ is held when it is time to vote.

Down

1. The ____ _____ takes over for the president if they die, resign or are impeached. (2 words)
2. An election is held every 4 years for this position in government. It is the highest rank in the executive branch and commander in chief of armed forces.
4. You cast your ____ during an election.

Things That Are Green!

Across
2. A cute, small fruit that is brown and fuzzy on the outside, but green and seeded on the inside.
6. This is a huge fruit that is green on the outside and bright red on the inside.

Down
1. A _____ is a what you get after you preserve a cucumber in a jar with vinegar and spices.
3. This usually grows in yards, parks and on golf courses.
4. ____s are more sour than lemons!
5. Poisonous _____ are very colorful and found in a jungle, but you can also find these green, hoppy amphibians in your own yard!

Gross!

Across
3. Throw up, puke or _____.
5. Gross things in your nose.
6. These will appear on your skin when time has passed after getting a cut or scrape.

Down
1. If you cut your skin deep enough, you might leak some _____.
2. This is what garbage is called when it is left around in public instead of being disposed of - also what you call a cat's bathroom!
4. These are weird creatures that move like snakes through soil. They are often used as bait to catch fish.

Halloween!

Across

2. This is a fun ride pulled by a tractor, but it might have a scratchy seat!
5. A mythical creature that has fangs, no reflection, and feeds on blood.
6. Special outfit you wear to look different than normal, sometimes not even human!

Down

1. "_____ or _____" is what you say to neighbors and friends when requesting goodies. (2 words)
3. These will be scooped out and carved.
4. A mythical creature that looks human until a full moon rises.

HOBBies!

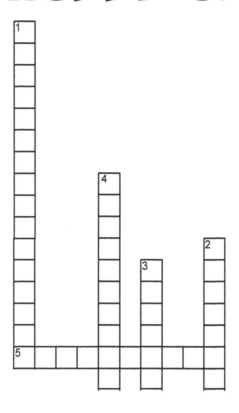

Across

5. If you have one of these, you like to gather similar items. Some people have a _____ of cards, dolls, jewelry or cars.

Down

1. Something almost everyone likes to do! People often enjoy _____ to _____ in the car, while dancing, or when they relax. (2 words)
2. _____ is a quiet activity that lets you discover different worlds! There are many different genres and authors to choose from.
3. Some people love physical activity! Some _____ include hockey, gymnastics, and football.
4. _____ _____ can be played on the computer, xBox, Playstation and more. (2 words)

Holidays in America!

Across
4. The _____ of ____ is often celebrated with a bang! Look to the sky for all the fireworks. (2 words)
6. A celebration for the end of December going into January. (2 words)

Down
1. Celebrated in October, this holiday can be spooky!
2. One of the biggest holidays of the year. This December holiday is celebrated by giving gifts to loved ones.
3. This holiday usually means a large feast: turkey, mashed potatoes, pumpkin pie and more!
5. This religious holiday often involves finding colorful dyed eggs.

Jewelry!

Across
2. Wear them on your ears.
4. Wear it on your finger.
5. Wear it around your neck.
6. Check the time with your wrist.

Down
1. Wear it around your wrist.
3. Wear it around your ankle.

Things to Keep clean!

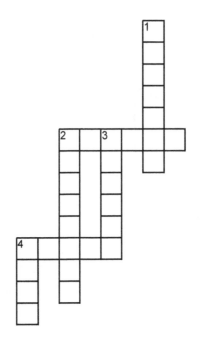

Across
2. These should be cleaned after every use because you eat food off of them.
4. You should always wash your _____ after using the restroom.

Down
1. Cleaning your _____, called doing laundry, is important because otherwise they can get very dirty and stained.
2. Sanitizing your _____s might be a good idea when someone is sick, because many people touch them when going between rooms throughout the day.
3. Keeping your _____ clean and free of objects is important so that no one trips on them while walking up or down.
4. Washing your _____ keeps it from becoming greasy and tangled.

In the Kitchen!

Across
4. You use this to wash dishes, wash your hands or rinse food.
5. If you don't want to wash dishes by hand, you can always use the _____.
7. This is where you toss things you don't want or need anymore (but not glass, cans or plastic)!
8. This is the area in the kitchen where you can set things down while you cook or prepare things.

Down
1. This keeps your food chilly, but not freezing.
2. This is what you use to eat; spoons, forks and knives are all types of _____.
3. These are where you can store food, plates or cups.
6. Using this machine, you can easily make smoothies!

Magical!

Across

3. A man with magical powers.
4. This is what you wave through the air when casting a spell!
5. A horse with a long, pointed and spiraled horn sticking out of its forehead.

Down

1. Witches love to create evil _____s in cauldrons.
2. Tinkerbell is one of these.
4. A lady with magical powers.

Food to Make at Home!

Across

3. This is a yummy lunch between two slices of bread.
5. Make this for a birthday treat and blow out the candles on top!

Down

1. Put fruit, juice and ice into a blender to make this healthy frozen drink.
2. Dip your corn chips into this yummy dip made from mashed avocados.
4. This comes in loaves and is usually sliced for toast.

Monsters!

Across
3. This monster has big fangs and feeds on blood! They have very white skin because they avoid sunlight.
5. This brain-eating monster will turn you into one of them if it bites or scratches you!
6. This might not have a real body, but it might scare you with their spirit or silhouette.

Down
1. This monster was brought alive by a mad scientist! He has metal bolts in his neck.
2. This will only come alive from the dead if you try to steal treasures from its tombs - it is all wrapped up.
4. This monster is a person by day, but turns into a terrifying wolf when the full moon rises.

Months!

Across

2. April showers bring what month's flowers?
5. This is usually the last month of summer break.
8. This month has a large feast at the end - Thanksgiving.
9. Love is in the air - Valentine's Day is in this month.
10. The beginning of summer!
11. This month starts with Labor Day weekend.
12. You might be fooled the first day of this month!

Down

1. The first month of the year.
3. You might go trick-or-treating at the end of this month.
4. The 4th of this month is celebrated with lots of fireworks.
6. The last month of the year.
7. If you're Irish, you might be celebrating St. Patrick's Day this month.

Monuments!

Across

2. In Chicago, IL, in the United States, you can find a giant silver ____,
3. In Egypt there are ancient pyramids, as well as the _____, which has the head of a human and the body of a lion.
5. In Paris, France, you will find a tall monument named the _____ Tower.

Down

1. This is a massive, ivory colored marble mausoleum in India. (2 words)
4. In New York, NY, in the United States, you can find the Statue of _____.

Noodles and Pasta!

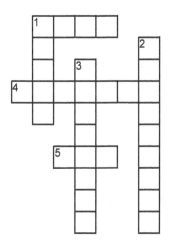

Across

1. Chicken noodle _____ is the perfect thing to eat when you feel sick.
4. This hearty meal is a dish with lots of layers all baked together. Ingredients include flat noodles with wavy edges, ricotta cheese, tomato sauce, and meat.
5. Stir ___ is often served over noodles or rice. It is a dish that originated in Asia and uses extremely hot oil to cook meat with vegetables in a wok.

Down

1. Pasta _____ is a delicious side dish that is served cold with multi-colored noodles, dressing, and other ingredients like tomatoes, olives, or onions.
2. This dish is a plate full of long, thin noodles with meatballs and tomato sauce on top.
3. _____ and cheese is most kids' favorite dish!

In the ocean!

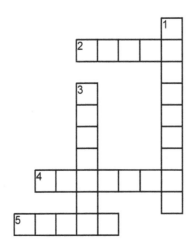

Across
2. This is the largest mammal on the planet.
4. An _____ has no bones, but does have 8 arms and a large, balloon-like head.
5. This carnivore is a huge fish with hundreds of sharp teeth.

Down
1. This soft aquatic animal has an umbrella shaped "body" with trailing tentacles that can sting.
3. This crustacean is often served in seafood restaurants - it has a tail, two large claws and is bright red after cooking.

Things in an Office!

Across
3. This device is used for talking to people, sending texts and/or e-mails, and plenty more!
4. An extra source of light that you can put on your desk.
5. This is a great tool to have at your side when you need 2 or more pieces of paper to be kept together.
6. A _____ is used to type information into a computer.

Down
1. This is a writing instrument. Be careful, it has no eraser!
2. In order to use a _____, you need a keyboard and a mouse.
3. A writing tool that is used when you might need to erase mistakes.

Types of Paint!

Across

3. This paint feels like plastic when it is dried and often has a thick texture.
5. These look like chalky tablets and need to be mixed with water.

Down

1. _____ paint comes in a handheld can with a nozzle.
2. _____ paint is fun for kids to use without a brush!
4. Fine artists throughout history have painted their masterpieces with ___ based paints.

Pets!

Across
2. This cute, hopping pet has really big ears.
3. A small, furry and cute rodent.
5. This animal is a long reptile with scales and no legs.

Down
1. This pet is fun to look at, but it must always remain in the water.
2. This animal might just fly away!
3. This pet is huge - it's even bigger than you. Big enough to ride!
4. This animal likes to meow.

Pretty Things!

Across

3. A tasty dessert! These tiny cakes are often decorated with colorful icing, sprinkles and more.
4. A pretty _____ is nice to watch in the evening on a beach.
5. ___ is a person's unique creation, such as a painting, drawing, sculpture, or other form.
6. Girls (and sometimes guys) wear this all the time. It's worn around the neck, wrist, finger, or other parts of the body.
7. This is a bride's outfit of the day. Probably white or off-white, this is the most glamorous _____ of her life!

Down

1. A bouquet of these pretty plants would melt anyone's heart!
2. These pretty bugs have many different colored wings.

64

Professions!

Across

5. This person will come to the rescue if there is a fire.

Down

1. This person's job is to make sure your body is healthy.
2. This is who helps you learn at school.
3. This person might work in a lab, use chemicals and do lots of research.
4. This is the person you go to in order to keep your teeth clean.

Things That Are Red!

Across
3. The most popular flower choice for Valentine's Day.
4. Be sure to come to a complete pause when driving as you come to a ____ ____. (2 words)
6. ____ is known as the "red planet".

Down
1. A ____, particularly a wild one, can be very dangerous and destructive if it isn't put out as soon as possible.
2. Bacon, lettuce and _____es make up BLT sandwiches.
5. You will get one if you don't wear sunscreen.

At a Restaurant!

Across

2. You look through a _____ when you are deciding what you want to order.
4. Your silverware often comes wrapped in a _____.
6. A female server.
7. Sometimes, if your family is very hungry and can't wait to eat, they will order an _____.

Down

1. This is what you ask for when you are ready to pay.
3. A male server.
5. Also called a gratuity, you pay this extra money to the server for doing their job. Normally it is an extra 15-25% of your total bill.

Rooms in a Home!

Across

3. This room is dedicated to eating meals. (2 words)
4. This room is at least partly underground and is the lowest level of a home.
5. This is where you sleep.

Down

1. This is the room where meals are cooked.
2. This is where your family probably has a couch and tv to relax and be together. (2 words)
4. This is the room where you brush your teeth and take showers or baths.

Royalty!

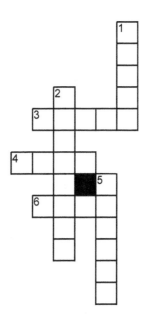

Across

3. A special head ornament worn by royalty to symbolize their honor, power and glory. This is often made with gold, diamonds and other jewels.
4. The highest level of royalty for a male.
6. The _____ to a throne is passed from king to queen, and queen to prince.

Down

1. The highest level of royalty for a female.
2. A _____ is the daughter of a king or queen.
5. A _____ is the son of a king or queen.

Shapes!

Across
5. A three sided shape.

Down
1. A shape with four sides that are perfectly equal to each other with right angles.
2. An eight-sided shape; the shape of a stop sign.
3. Just like a "decade" is 10 years, a _____ has 10 sides.
4. This is a shape but not a polygon. It has no "sides".

Things in the Sky!

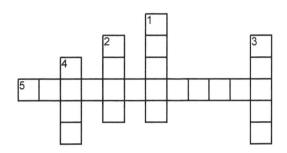

Across

5. To see a _____ _____ is rare. You need to be looking at the night sky at just the right time or you might miss it! (2 words)

Down

1. You are very likely to see lots of _____s near airports.
2. You might have one of these! It can fly high on a windy day.
3. These are everywhere! They fly in the sky and you might have one as a pet.
4. This may look small but it's actually huge and orbits the Earth.

Snacks!

Across
4. This could be a snack or a meal. Just stick something between two slices of bread!
5. This is what you get when you heat up dried kernels of corn.
6. Cashews, pistachios, almonds and pecans are all types of ____.
7. These baked, brown, and salty snacks are all twisted! They can be soft or crunchy.

Down
1. This kind of snack could be an apple, pear, orange, or a banana.
2. This rectangular snack is full of oats and sometimes has added nuts or chocolate chips. (2 words)
3. This snack is made by deep frying thin slices of potatoes.

SPace!

Across
1. The sun, moon and all our nearest planets are part of this. (2 words)
2. This white circle in the sky can sometimes be seen during the day, but most often at night.
4. Some people believe these other life forms are out in the universe, but they aren't on our planet!
5. This is what we call our solar system's star.

Down
1. If you are lucky, you might see this fly across the sky on a clear night. (2 words)
3. The name of the galaxy we call our home. (2 words)

SPorts!

Across
3. A game played on ice involving sticks and a puck.
6. A sport that can be played indoors and outdoors - all you need is a ball and a hoop.

Down
1. Primarily a women's sport, this involves lots of dancing, balance and cheering.
2. A famous sport played on a diamond. Equipment includes balls and a bat.
4. The U.S. name for this world-famous sport played on a field using a ball and a net for making goals. Other countries call it football.
5. This involves a lot of balance and coordination. Balance bars, parallel beams and mats are often used.

Spring!

Across

2. Not all of spring is warm; sometimes you might wake up to a layer of _____ on the car or ground.
6. This mini vacation from school is typically a week long. (2 words)

Down

1. Spring is when people begin their _____ work for the year so that they can have nice flowers and food growing in the summer.
2. _____ are nice to look at in a garden or in a vase.
3. Thunderstorms will make a lot of this fall from the sky.
4. The month known for lots of rain showers.
5. The month known for lots of flowers.

St. Patrick's Day!

Across

2. St. Patrick's Day is always on _____ 17th.
4. Who doesn't want a pot of ____?
6. A _____ is usually portrayed as a gnome with red hair wearing green clothes.

Down

1. St. Patrick's Day is a holiday that originates from the country of _____.
3. A small green 3 or 4 leaf clover.
4. The color of the day!
5. Legend says there is a pot of gold at the end of the _____.

Staying Healthy!

Across
3. These are a sweet type of food that are picked from trees and bushes.
6. Plants you can eat - sometimes you eat the leaves, sometimes the roots!

Down
1. You should be sure to floss and brush ____ _____ after you wake up and before you go to sleep. (2 words)
2. It's important to wash ____ _____ before eating and after using the restroom.
4. You get this at the doctor in the form of a shot. It will protect you from catching harmful diseases!
5. Stay hydrated! Drink eight, 8-ounce glasses of _____ each day.

Summer!

Across

2. A trip to the _____ is always nice because you can swim, play in the sand, or just lay in the warm sun.
3. Going to the ___ is fun because you get to see and learn about hundreds of different animals!
7. Lots of people like to get away from home and go on a _____ during the summer.

Down

1. A popular refreshing drink made from a yellow, sour fruit.
4. Some people will take a ____ ____, meaning they will drive a long distance while making some stops along the way. (2 words)
5. _____ is fun because even if you aren't good at moving your body through water, you can always use floaties or inner tubes!
6. If you don't protect yourself from the sun, you might get a _____.

Sun Protection!

Across

1. This type of protective lotion reflects most of the sun's rays before they enter your skin, but it lets some pass through.
4. Wear this fabric on your body to prevent a sunburn.

Down

1. Wear these in front of your eyes.
2. Wear this on your head to protect your scalp.
3. This protective lotion reflects all of the sun's rays so that none of them enter your skin.

Things You Can't See!

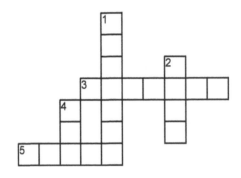

Across

3. This keeps everything down on Earth.
5. You should protect yourself from these bad microscopic organisms so you don't get sick.

Down

1. Some people claim to have seen these spooky beings, but it is widely debated if they truly exist.
2. You can see trees leaning, hats flying and leaves swirling. What you don't see is the _____ itself moving them.
4. You breathe this all day, every day.

Time!

Across

3. There are 24 of these per day.
6. The twelfth hour of the day is commonly referred to as ____.
7. This is normally when people eat dinner.

Down

1. It is common for kids to get out of school in the _____.
2. Just a _____!
4. This consists of only 60 seconds.
5. Typically, people wake up and start their day in the _____.

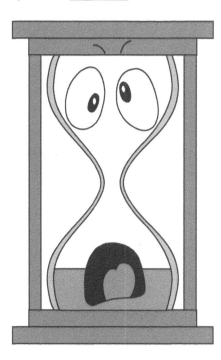

Transportation!

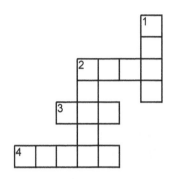

Across

2. This vehicle service is handy when you need another person to drive you somewhere.
3. This is a vehicle many people own and take to work or school each day.
4. You might see one of these if you look up to the sky at just the right time.

Down

1. This vehicle is a super-sized boat that can hold hundreds of people.
2. This is a fast moving vehicle that has many links and travels on rails.

Trees!

Across
2. This tree has small, very sweet red fruits that can top a sundae.
3. This is the kind of tree that is decorated for Christmas.
4. If you want to make cider, consider picking _____s right off the tree!

Down
1. A tree that is green all year long.
3. These trees are common in the tropics and some grow coconuts.

Valentine's Day!

Across
3. Valentine's Day is a celebration of _____.
4. Valentine's Day is always on _____ 14th.
6. The most popular symbol of this holiday! You also have one in your body.
7. A sweet treat given as gifts - it often comes in heart shaped boxes.

Down
1. Will you be _____?
2. A good way to enjoy this day is a _____ date or dinner with the love of your life.
5. Just like chocolate, a bouquet of these flowers would make a great gift.

Veggies!

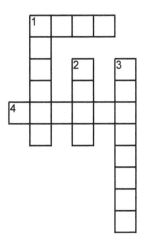

Across
1. A yellow veggie with lots of kernels.
4. Some people consider this red, round and soft veggie to be a fruit because it has seeds inside.

Down
1. Bright orange, this veggie is long and pointed.
2. These veggies grow in pods. When you eat a spoonful of them, you are probably eating 10 at a time.
3. This veggie looks like a tiny tree: green with branches.

Weather!

Across

3. This falls from the sky more slowly than rain, and if you catch some, you can see each tiny flake.
4. This disasterous storm is known as a cyclone or typhoon in other parts of the world. It is many miles wide and has an "eye" in the center.
5. This storm condition will leave you swimming if you don't reach higher ground!

Down

1. This is a common wet weather disturbance that does not usually cause damage, but it can be very loud.
2. This terrible disaster spins and spins and destroys everything in its path.
4. This precipitation would not be fun to walk through: tiny flying balls of ice!

Whales & Dolphins!

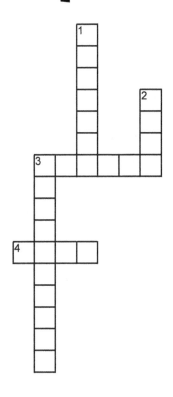

Across

3. This unique whale has a very large forehead, no dorsal fin and is all-white in color.
4. The _____ whale is named after a color.

Down

1. This type of whale is possibly the most unique - it looks like an underwater unicorn!
2. Also known as a killer whale, this creature is black and white and is actually the largest species of dolphin.
3. One of the most familiar types of dolphins. It is named for the shape of its nose.

Where Is It?

Across

5. Emperor penguins breed during the coldest time in the coldest place on Earth: winter in _____.

Down

1. The Great Barrier Reef, off the coast of _____, is home to over 1,500 different species of fish.
2. The capital city of this country is New Delhi, and it is also home to the Taj Mahal.
3. Tropical fish are found in the _____ near the equator.

Winter!

Across

2. This is an ice formation that often develops on the edges of houses. It can be very long and sharp.
4. You might see this white stuff covering your grass the morning after a freezing night.
5. You might wear these to keep your ears warm. (2 words)
6. Put these on your hands to keep them warm. One pocket for your fingers and one for your thumbs.

Down

1. These will keep your hands warm; one pocket for each finger and thumb.
3. A big holiday near the end of December.

STUMPED?

The answer keys for all the Puzzles in this Book Can Be found at:

http://www.woojr.com/kiDs-CrossworD-answers/

Visit WWW.WOOjr.com

for hundreds more screen-free kids crafts, teacher worksheets, family-friendly recipes, and printable activities all year round!